Critique of Hope

DR. ORTRUN SCHULZ, born 1960 in Hannover, Germany. Master of Arts in Philosophy and English Linguistics 1986, PhD in Philosophy 1993. From 1992 until 2005 editor of *Schopenhauer-Jahrbuch*. Private research and various publications.

Hope is a basic affection of the mind. This philosophical analysis will clarify the concept by dealing with its involvement in knowledge, ethics and metaphysics. Being a belief, oscillating between knowledge and ignorance, hope is prone to illusion and disappointment. Man can be guided and manipulated by hope. Therefore its role within ideology and enlightenment will be investigated. We will reflect on whether and when hope may be a blessing or an evil, and on how intellectual freedom is possible.

Ortrun Schulz

Critique of Hope

Bibliographical information of the German national library: http://dnb.dnb.de

© 2018 Ortrun Schulz

Printing and Production: BoD - Books on Demand, Norderstedt, Germany

ISBN 978-3-7528-2383-7

That thou mayest be able to spend thy life smoothly
Let not everpressing desire torment and vex thee,
Or fear or hope for things of little worth.

(Horace (65 B.C. - 8 B.C.), *Epistulae*, I, 18, 97)[1]

Contents

Introduction

Recently, the American TV series "Dr. Phil Show" broadcasted the case of a dating scam where an elderly wealthy gentleman, Dennis, sent $ 250,000 via Western Union over a period of several months between 2016 and 2017 to a supposedly pretty American woman named Kimberly Escobar, who was allegedly stranded without funds, first in South Africa, then in Turkey and finally in Amsterdam. There was a rude awakening for him when it turned out that the photo of another person had been stolen and the whole profile was a fake. The betrayed man had become not only the victim of a "catfish", but at the same time a victim of his own hope.

An elderly divorced woman, with the help of money she borrowed from friends and relatives, even sent nearly one and a half million dollars between 2013 and 2015 to a scammer posing as Chris Olsen, a stunningly handsome Italian-American widower, who she believed was on a business trip in South Africa.

Many of these dating scammers are Nigerians who assume a false identity online or even by phone and invent touching stories of distress.

The methods of the telephone mafia of some call centers are based on the same principle. People are being called and told that they have, for example, won 39,000 and would need to advance bank charges to complete the transaction. If the gullible falls for it, he receives another call and learns that the number had accidentally been twisted and he actually won 93,000 and therefore would have to settle a larger sum in advance. Although this scam is already well known, many still fall for it.

In many cases, the victims of hope are unaware of the exploitation. In 1992 I met a retired old lady in Australia who was traveling the country and staying in youth hostel dormitories. On the one hand she did that to save money, as she did her trade trips at her own expense, on the other hand to meet more potential buyers as she sold diet products of a company. The driving force behind her action was the prospect of taking part in the draw for above-average sales performance for a one-week trip to Singapore.

Own image

The amazingly honest program of this company said that there were "only 2 types of people. 1. Non dreamers –

11

people who have accepted to remain average! 2. Dreamers [...]." It seems that there is no self-misunderstanding, because the misled understand themselves as dreamers. But they misjudge the likelihood of gaining success and overestimate their abilities. They are indoctrinated by the marketing strategy of such a "mission statement" to hold dreams for a value, and they consider it more likely subjectively than it is objectively that their dream be fulfilled. Behind this is the deliberate disregard of ethical guidelines for communication on the part of those responsible. It is deliberate manipulation of others for their own sake. This is illustrated in the well-known image of the so-called "carrot on a stick motivation", where a donkey runs behind the carrot, which his driver holds on a stick from behind in front of the donkey's mouth. The reward is always just out of reach, so that the alleged promise in reality is none, and is also referred to as a "lie" in game theory.

Drawing by Rita and Ortrun Schulz

The motive here is mere hope, which is not fulfilled and still acts as an engine of exploitation. This motivational strategy is by no means identical to the "carrot and whip" method, in which reward and punishment actually materialize. Hope has an interactive-ethical component. Because creating and nourishing false or unrealistic hopes in other people violates the rules of ethical communication. To be truthful and to keep promises are actions that involve the purpose of not disappointing others. Those affected may then hope that the other will keep his word to them, which constitutes a substantial basis of trust in the community. To raise false expectations and to support others' unjustified or poorly justified hopes is often based on self-interest in order to manipulate them according to one's own interests. Their possible subsequent disappointment is endorsed, thus is contributing to their psychic injury. He who lightheartedly fosters hopes that do not come true, hurts the other. Not to deceive others falls into the field of ethics of communication. Intellectual honesty with oneself, on the other hand, belongs to an ethics of belief.

Hope can be more or less well-grounded, but this is difficult to judge, since an essential concomitant of hope is ignorance, even "blindness", as expressed in the symbolic oil painting "Hope" by the English painter George Frederic Watts.

https://commons.wikimedia.org/wiki/File:
George_Frederic_Watts,_1885,_Hope.jpg[3]

There are several versions of the painting, and this is the first one from 1885. A girl with a blindfold sits on a globe and plays on a lyre with only one string left. It shows impressively how weak the reasons are to believe.

Hope is life's promise of happiness. Thinking clings almost like a reflex to what is uplifting, pleasant and agreeable. The analysis of the human condition reveals the struggle for goals along the way of the fundamental aim for self-preservation. There are needs and wants, and possible ways to meet them or not. These relations usually involve problems which are mentally represented as various states between security and doubt, hope and despair. Taken in the context of our existence, talking about hope involves questions of truth and error, desire and probability, expectation and faith.

1. Traditional Views

Being at the core of human existence, the concept of hope has been dealt with since antiquity. In ancient Greece the term of "hope" (*elpis*) corresponds roughly to "expectation". It refers to an unspecific future dimension.

Skeptical or even negative connotations concerning expectation are expressed by Pindar (522 or 518 B.C. - 446 B.C.) and Hesiod (born before 700 B.C.). They do not have high esteem of its subjective bias. Pindar mentions the "envious and greedy expectations of the mortals", which are nothing but selfish imaginations. Hesiod talks about "empty hope" or the futility of an optimistic expectation, for which no effort is made, and which is likely to eventually turn out to have been an illusion.

The ambivalence as to whether hope should be considered a plague or a good is reflected in the various versions of the *Pandora fable*. According to Hesiod, Zeus sends Pandora to earth with a jar filled with *evils*, and they all get released except the last one, hope. But in the version of Babrius, the jar contains *goods*, which all escape and only one, hope, is retained as consolation for man. Schopenhauer suspects that originally the jar contained goods as reported by Babrius and that the myth was either misunderstood or deliberately changed by Hesiod[4]

The uncertainty of the future and the randomness of events, without obvious relation to human wishes and fates, result in a rather skeptical attitude towards hope, especially in the tragic poetry and Stoicism of Aeschylus (525 B.C. - 456 B.C.) and Sophocles (497/496 B.C. - 406/405 B.C.).

Distinct from this, however, there is also an emphasis on a rational justification for assuming a desirable course of future events. Herodotus (490/480 B.C. - around 424 B.C.) and Thucydides (before 454 B.C. - between 399 B.C. and 396 B.C.) consider a well-founded hopeful assumption to be legitimate. Democritus (460/459 B.C – ca. 371 B.C.) distinguishes between the correct prognoses made by people with insight, and the impossible expectations of ignorant people.[5]

A merely probable prognosis, however, is not necessarily grounds for an expectation of a happy ending, as is typical for hope. This meaning, "a trust in positive future possibilities guided by subjective interest", can be found for the first time in Sophocles (497/496 B.C. - 406/405 B.C).

So we have discovered three main aspects of the meaning of "expectation" in archaic and classical antiquity:
1.   Illusionary belief
2.   Rational prognosis
3.   Existential trust.[6]

Plato (428/427 B.C. - 348/347 B.C.) calls hope, desire and anticipation the soul's grips on future things, differentiating between good and bad, true and false expectations. Plato fosters a concept of hope which transcends the sensual world, and reaches its true destination only in the world of pure ideas, in view of the true, the beautiful and the good. This meaning is also included in Hellenistic and late antique religion.

Aristotle (384 B.C. - 322 B-C.) emphasizes the rational aspect of expectation, and describes a "science of prognosis." Like fear, he also considers hope as an *affection*. Fear is a depressed state; hope an uplifted state of the soul.[7]

In the *Old Testament* the concept of expectation clearly has the meaning of hope regarding the promised– good – future. Unlike the Greek rational prognosis, in the sense of an extrapolation from the present and its conditions, Jewish hope aims faithfully above reality at an eschatology, or end of time - the coming of the Messiah, the kingdom of God. Prudence advises to "avoid catching the wind" (Koheleth).

Christian hope is defined by the apostle Paul as "trust in God who raises the dead."

For Augustine (395 – 430) hope means neither an uncertain expectation, nor hope for a future worldly good, but a transcendent one. The meaning of life becomes to live so that one merits a place in Heaven, or at least to make oneself worthy of God's grace. Augustine lists hope, together with faith and love, as the cardinal Christian virtues or commandments.

Faith, love and hope were personified as daughters of Saint Sophia, the personification of wisdom. Representations of Fides, Caritas and Spes as three saintly women became known in the West as early as the 6th century and were common in France and Luxembourg, but also in the Rhineland.[8]

St. Sophia with her three daughters,
statue around 1870, chapel at Castle
Löwenstein, Kleinheubach[9]

The defamation of doubt and despair is the downside to the explicit or implicit duty of happiness. Who is dissatisfied, may be considered godless. For example, sadness (*tristitia*) is one of the deadly sins of the Middle Ages. Despair is considered a sin like doubt and hybris by Chrysostomos (349 or 344 – 407). Even as late as 1849, Kierkegaard calls it a fatal illness. Many Christian theologians regard despair as arbitrary anticipation of the non-fulfillment of God's promise.

In the Christian Middle Ages the act of hoping (*spes qua)* is distinguished from the goal of hope (*spes quae*). The former is an affect which contains a pleasurable expectation of a future reality and has different degrees of intensity and certainty.[10] Thomas Aquinas (ca. 1225 - 1274) describes hope as a "striving motion", directed towards a possible future good.[11]

The reformer Martin Luther (1483 - 1546) points out the difference between the general human hope in regard to an actual situation, and Christian hope growing from the believer's faith. Apocalyptic thoughts play a minor role in him, but continue in the historical development in various intellectual currents.

In the 17th and 18th century hope and fear are grouped together, and are treated within the theories of affects and politics, such as those of Thomas Hobbes, René Descartes und Baruch Spinoza. Hobbes Hobbes (1588 - 1679) mentions in his main work *Leviathan* that men can be manipulated by hope and fear.

Each of these is defined as a passion (lat. *passio*). As long as the intellect receives impressions, it remains passive. The term "passion" reveals this etymology. Descartes (1596 - 1650) claims the freedom of will and unlimited power of the mind over the affects. Hope may involve a false judgment. Unwarranted hope is an error, which results from one's will or faculty of affirmation expanding further than what the intellect understands clearly and distinctly. Overriding passions make us slaves and should be overcome.

Descartes observes that the mere thought of a good within our reach would be stimulus enough for us to desire it. If we believe in a sufficient probability of obtaining it, then we are filled with hope. If hope becomes strong enough, its nature changes, and is called "confidence."[12]

His follower Spinoza (1632 - 1677) claims the strife for self-preservation as basic principle and origin of all affects. According to him this force is the essence of man, as well as everything else. Man tends to imagine pleasant things as real.[13]

He defines hope as an unstable joy, resulting from an idea of some future or past thing, in an outcome about which we are in doubt.[14] Due to uncertainty in our reflection on this outcome's degree of probability, both the affections of joy and sadness are involved. This oscillating condition accounts for hope being a kind of pain, in a similar way as fear. None of them could be good.[15]

Moreover, these affects contain a lack of knowledge and an impotence of the mind, and therefore are signs of mental weakness. The free man stands beyond hope and fear.[16] In his attempt to mimic the geometrical method of reasoning, Spinoza says that the greater the fear of an evil, the greater must be the corresponding hope to avoid it, because these affects are proportionate to each other.

The causes for the formation of a political state are hope and fear. The hope for security is primary, since positive thinking is not the exception but the norm. Our nature is to "readily believe what we hope, but hardly believe what we fear, and of both more or less than would be appropriate."[17] People can be governed by these affects, but once hope and fear are gone, man is free.[18]

David Hume (1711-1776) discusses the affects in the Second Book of his *Treatise of Human Nature* published anonymously in 1739-40. Included are sorrow and joy, hope and fear. He poses the thesis that "reason is only a slave of the passions."

Later discussions of hope are actually mere variations of the previous definitions and evaluations, sometimes with concretizations of particular objects of hope, i.e. beliefs. Therefore, I do not treat them in this chapter anymore, but will integrate them into the following ones.

2. The Passion of Hope

Hope was already described in great detail by Spinoza in his theory of affections. Based on Spinoza's definition, Gabriel Marcel (1889 - 1973) points out that hope is the cognitive primary affect in man. "Hope may well be the fabric of which our souls are made."[19] Ernst Bloch (1885 - 1977) calls hope the most human of all mental states, a human's basic affect. For him, hope is a "principle" as well as an affection, which intends a forward expansion of the self into some utopia.[20]

Schopenhauer (1788-1860), the great pessimist and metaphysician of the blind will, actually founded his entire philosophy on a critique of hope. Therefore, the present work contains numerous references to him. In his remarks on hope he also relies on traditional views.

The affect of hope can be either an emotion or a passion. *Affections* are all stirrings of the will, while *emotions* are momentary reactions, and *passions* last longer. Passions also lack certainty of knowledge, and distort the objective apprehension of reality. Hope is usually ranked among the passions because it often involves something like an attitude which makes hope more persistent than a fleeting emotion.

Passion is an inclination so strong, that the motives that excite it exercise a power which is stronger than that of any possible motive acting against them. Its mastery over our will thus becomes absolute; consequently, the attitude of the will towards it is passive, an attitude of suffering.

Emotion is a stirring of the will, just as irresistible as a passion yet only temporary. It takes away intellectual freedom, because not all motives can be contemplated in the same manner. Rational judgment is overrun and rendered "passive", being swept away like in a tsunami. The conflict between impulse and thought is a constant challenge for man. He has a choice between giving in to temptation or self-control, spontaneity or deliberation.

The emotions are also vehicles of illusions. They lead to faulty thinking because they obstruct clear sight and thought. They glare, and make us biased. We see only what we want to see, and nothing else. Objects appear differently from what they are, or how we would apprehend them in a different state of mind. The strength of impressions depends on the strength of emotional arousal.

Every event which causes an unpleasant emotion will leave a lasting effect in our mind, even if it is trifling. As long as it lingers it will obstruct the clear, objective grasp of things and circumstances. It will even tinge all of our thoughts, like a tiny object brought close to our eye distorts our vision.[21]

A special role is played by closeness in time, in affectively loaded reactions. Emotions rely on the present moment, during which they mainly exist just like the will. This intensity fades over time. Small objects in space appear big when close, but turn small and insignificant when further away. It is similar with objects in time. The events and accidents taking place in our daily lives appear important to us as long as they are present or close in time. They cause us all sorts of emotions. But as soon as the flux of time has moved them further away, they become insignificant, not worthy of any attention and soon forgotten, because their apparent size was based on nothing but their proximity.[22]

Every intense joy is mixed with bitterness because it is transient, and bonds man on the wheel of fortune. Fortune is futile and can change any moment. Once out of luck, loss is suffered and grief results. Unfulfilled hope is followed by the affect of disappointment. Shattered hope hits with violence. The greater the preceding hope was, the greater is the negative affect of sadness or anger and the feeling of emptiness. The term "dis-appointment" suggests the absence of an expected appointment. Hope contains the possibility of error, because it is directed towards an uncertain future. Hope implies an inadequate idea, because it assumes something as true which later turns out to be false. This inadequate idea accounts for the risk factor in hoping. A life of hope is a life of risk. But perhaps only a life with risk is real life, and who does not hope anymore, does not really live anymore.

Animals are less bothered by the unpleasant concern for their maintenance and the uncertainties of hope. But maybe their lives are therefore poorer in joy since hope anticipates a happier future. This vivid imagination is the source of man's greatest joy and pleasure, which animals lack. They could therefore be called "hopeless." However, it is just this trait, the fact that they live in the moment, which makes animals display greater calmness and serenity.[23]

But man does not get "the joys of hope and anticipation" for free. Namely, what somebody enjoys through hope and expectation is later deducted from the real event, as it turns out less satisfactorily than expected.[24]

2.1. Bribed Reason and Folly of the Heart

> *Hope* makes us regard what we desire, and *fear* what we are afraid of, as being probable and near, and both magnify their object.[25]

The imperfections of the intellect are much increased by the disturbances of the will. Every passion as well as every like or dislike tinges the objects of knowledge and blurs the image. Reason is bribed by hope or blinded by fear.[26]

Humans are more prone to error and falsehood than animals: man is a liar through and through, cheating both himself and others. These masks, illusions and errors result from the influence of the will on the intellect. Schopenhauer thinks that logic is practically useless since *wrong conclusions* are very rare. But *wrong judgments* are most common, and logic does not help at all to correct them.

In Psychology, Schopenhauer establishes a so-called Copernican turn after an earlier model. Nicolaus Copernicus formulated a heliocentric model in the Renaissance. He claimed that it is not the sun which revolves around the earth, but that the earth revolves around the sun. Kant applied this idea of a turn to his theory of knowledge and claimed that experience is constituted by subjective conditions.

Schopenhauer uses a turn, too. He turns around the master and servant relationship in the mind. Unlike in the past, where the intellect was thought to reign, it now becomes the will to live. From this can be concluded that the will corrupts almost every step of the intellect. [27]

Schopenhauer's criticism of the "bribed reason" has a long tradition. We should mention Francis Bacon and his theory of idols as well as René Descartes and Baruch Spinoza in the 17th century with their aim to deconstruct the prejudices, and finally Immanuel Kant and his critique of reason in order to determine its limits. The question of how far the competence of reason goes is the main theme in an ideological conflict.

For Schopenhauer reason is corrupted, namely bribed by interest in one's own advantage. "Thus is our intellect daily befooled and corrupted by the deceptions of inclination and liking."[28] Emotions and affections are reactions to this kind of satisfaction or dissatisfaction of the will, and falsify our judgments.

Despite their differences, Schopenhauer agrees with Descartes insofar as for him also, faulty judgments are caused by extensive and unrestricted use of the faculty of affirmation or "will". Errors happen when belief kicks in too early without clear and distinct comprehension. There is a will to believe, especially with regard to hope. The intellect's calculation of the probability is overrun by an act of will.

Given its natural origin, the intellect is primarily a tool in the struggle for survival. The interests of life influence its performance in many ways. It is extremely difficult to get a clear picture of anything in which we are interested. It is hardly possible, since the will immediately interferes with every argument and every added data. The voice of the will cannot easily be distinguished from the voice of the intellect, because both are merged into *one*, the ego. This is manifested especially whenever we want to make a guess on the outcome of something. Here interest falsifies almost every move of the intellect, be it as fear, be it as hope. It is hardly possible to see clearly, because the intellect resembles a torch for reading which is flickering in a strong breeze.[29]

When the intellect's probability calculus is disturbed by wishful thinking, hope results.

> *Hope* is to confuse the desire that something should occur with the probability that it will. Perhaps no man is free from this folly of the heart, which deranges the intellect's correct estimation of probability to such a degree as to make him think the event quite possible, even if the chances are only a thousand to one. [30]

The unwarranted anticipation of satisfaction comes directly from the influence of willing in the representation. Not only are the real perspectives weighed, but the objectively unlikely scenario is believed to be probable. Desire anticipates the wanted object or event and represents the future joy, but without actually feeling it because it is blended with painful doubt and uncertainty. The present involves the feeling of something lacking which is not yet achieved, and this inflicts some discomfort.

Hope is wishful thinking and as such, one-sided. The origin of hope out of desire leads to a wrong assessment of the situation, and can even make one mentally blind.

> What is opposed to our part, our plan, our wish, or our hope often cannot possibly be grasped and comprehended by us, whereas it is clear to the eyes of everyone else; on the other hand, what is favorable to these leaps to our eyes from afar. What opposes the heart is not admitted by the head.[31]

The origin of hope from desire leads to a misjudgment of the situation. Thus, hope is not only partially "blind" as far as the part of ignorance in it is concerned, but it also makes us blind as love does, for all its opposing reasons. This is the meaning of the blindfold in the painting "Hope".

2.2. Fuel for the Mind and Motive of Action

Hope and even more so, optimism may encourage some kind of inertia. Marcel says "the technician, inventor or researcher" is looking for ways and means and may be confident in finding it, but the hopeful person simply says, "It'll be alright."[32] The shallow optimist may even abstain from any efforts and avoid proper measures to prevent disaster.

However, it is not always the case that the activity of the will has a purely negative impact on thinking. Bacon uses a metaphor, that the intellect is a light which receives oil to burn from the will and the passions.[33] Memory and performance can be enhanced by interest. The spur of the will can work as an incentive. It may support the intellect.[34]

Positive anticipation often functions as incentive for action. This is why hope is often considered indispensable for any success. It is not always necessary to have a clear idea or anticipation of what is being hoped for.

Hope can be unspecific. Hoping for a miracle may be lifesaving. The following fable was originally written by the Greek poet Aesop (600 B.C. - 564 B.C.) around 550 B.C. A frog whose pond had dried out was hopping around a farmyard. In the barn he discovered a pail half-filled with fresh milk and when looking in he slipped and fell in. Since the sides of the pail were too steep and the bottom too deep he could not get out again. For many hours he was frantically kicking and squirming getting very exhausted, until at last the milk had turned into a solid hunk of butter and he could jump out of the pail.

Own image; frog
http://clipartmag.com/frogs-clipart#frogs-clipart-36.jpg

Bloch summarizes the ambivalence of hope's worth: False hope is one of the biggest evils of mankind, but true hope is its greatest blessing.[35]

The loss of hope can lead to despair in man. Hopelessness is forced upon him and is an unnatural condition. Despair can create a subjective hell if somebody clearly recognizes the aim of his willing and also realizes that he can never reach it, but nevertheless keeps willing it. If the object of desire is so unreachable that there is no hope left to ever attain it, then despair enters.

In Dante's *Divine Comedy* (1472) a line "in dark letters" at the entrance to hell reads: "Give up hope all ye enter here."[36]. This suggests that hopelessness is the entrance to hell. The sinners' souls are condemned to remain restless forever: "No hope will give them strength to gain peace of mind or ease their pain."[37]

It can be assumed that in response to the Gate to Hell, the "Gate of Hope" was created by Ewald Mataré (1887-1965) in 1957/58. It is the right bronze door on the portal of the Salzburg Cathedral:

https://commons.wikimedia.org/wiki/File:
Salzburger_Dom_Tor_der_Hoffnung_Ewald_
Mataré_080320153652.jpg[38]

3. The Goals of Hope

The object classes of hope can be divided into world immanent and transcendent. However, hope always transcends the given. It crosses the factual by a vision of something better, either as world-immanent, that is a hope for worldly goods, or as a transcendent or religious hope for heaven. [39]

For all the variety of objects, it is true for all that as long as we hope for something, the hoped-for seems to us to be significant. We are not indifferent. The worthiness of what is hoped for lifts the corresponding object out of indifference.[40]

The object of desire receives a positive rating or is regarded as a good. Spinoza and Schopenhauer both reverse the order in this relationship, contrary to traditional view. We would not aspire, want, crave, or desire anything because we think it is good, but we think something is good because we seek, want, desire, and wish it.[41] But while there is certainly a dependency, it is unlikely that such a chronological order can always be assumed. Advertising often arouses our desire and suggests things as good, which we only strive for afterwards.

3.1. Worldly Happiness

Objects of desire, and thus the hope of obtaining them, are manifold in their content. Most hope to find the right partner, win the lottery, stay healthy and more. In form, however, the personal aspirations of the individual can be summarized succinctly with Schopenhauer: everyone wants existence, well-being and procreation.

Nosce te ipsum, "know yourself" – when this saying was engraved above the entrance of the Temple of Apollo in Delphi, self-knowledge was already considered a difficult requirement for philosophical thought. The call originally came from Thales (after others: Cheilon). For Socrates self-knowledge was the precondition of virtue, for Lessing the "center of all wisdom," for Kant "the beginning of all human wisdom." Enlightenment about oneself is an indispensable part of life wisdom and a basic requirement for happiness. You have to know your interests and know what you want.

Happiness and joy are the primary objects of hope for this life, and accordingly one hopes to avert their opposites, namely unhappiness and grief. The greatest thinkers in human history have tried to remedy suffering, and a mind storm has been unleashed against grief. Ludwig Marcuse aptly says, "Spinoza thinks to be happy."[42]

Spinoza, to put it succinctly, argues the thesis that knowledge makes one happy.[43] But why? At first only with people who like to think. And that knowledge is not a lasting, inalienable happiness for which he sought, escaped him. He overlooked forgetfulness. Nietzsche notes cynically: "Blessed are the forgetful ones: for they are finished even with their stupidities."[44]

Spinoza's move in his *Ethics* relies on the relatively easy remedy for passivity which he identifies with suffering. Similar to later Freud, Spinoza claims, that if we recognize the causes of sadness, it ceases to be a state of suffering, and so far, it stops being sad.[45]

According to this view, happiness would have to be achieved through knowledge, even the realization of the misfortune. But the power of knowledge, in comparison to the power of facts, is generally poor. Of course, knowing is more readily available, and with it the happiness of knowing. It depends on you. Spinoza wants to turn the wheel of Fortune himself. Since objects are represented and I am the agent involved in their constitution, it should be easier to change my attitude than the objects.

But what is gained by the change of passivity to activity? Is freedom from outside determination in the mind already freedom from suffering? Even if knowledge is exhilarating, it is always only attached to suffering. The same criticism applies to the assumption made by today's psychotherapy, that knowledge of suffering already cures it. If only the cause of the depression were recognized, it would disappear; instead of fixing the reason. But it is the insatiable longing which constitutes suffering. Desire can not be defeated by being rationalistically suppressed: it remains resistant to all reason; it is the will on which reason rebounds and despairs. Certainly, for Spinoza activity is perfection, and passivity is impotence and as such aversion.

Marcuse notes that this figure of thought is already found in Thomas Aquinas' non-distinction between receiving and suffering, according to which, in the *Summa Theologica*, every sorrow, which is a subspecies of suffering, could be "appeased by a pleasure."[46]

The crusaders against grief claimed that sadness was harmful, or morbid (black bile). The diagnosticians of the bad were discredited by all means or, most effectively, ignored: He who puts the dark into the light, is put into the dark.[47]

For the sufferer is exemplified Old Testament Job, the just man who lost everything. In this biblical story it becomes clear how out of place and insensitive arguments are in distress. In the ears of Job, arguments are not very comforting. And even though rational thinking is often the only way to address suffering, philosophical reason does not have the power over the existence or non-existence of pain. And the insight into the futility of argumentative consolation leads the philosopher to see himself in dust and ashes, no longer musing over their whence and why, but considering his place in this dust and ashes.[48]

The situation in which Job finds himself is a particular problem in religion, because from the standpoint of religion it seems scandalous and incomprehensible why God makes a good person suffer. The sun shines on the righteous and the unrighteous. But even without this link with morality, suffering is a problem in every life. Buddhism says that all life is suffering. Suffering is the denser reality.

> Of course, as Schiller says, we are all born to Arcadia; in other words, we come into the world full of claims of happiness and pleasure and cherish the foolish hope of making them good. As a rule, however, fate soon comes along, seizes us harshly and roughly, and teaches us that nothing belongs to *us* but everything to *it*, since it has undisputed right not only to all our possessions and acquisitions, to wife and family, but even to our arms and legs, our eyes and ears, and to the very nose in the middle of our face.[49]

Job is thrown to the one extreme of human life, which is misery, the one whose other pole is boredom. Sorrow and pain arise from the discrepancy between aspiration and achievement. Pain is thwarted will. Remembering what has been lost, worrying about the future or hoping for happiness are enormous means of increasing suffering.[50]

We appreciate our goods only when we have lost them. For happiness is fleeting and usually consists in the removal of want and pain. So we usually find the pleasures far below, the pain far beyond our expectation.[51]

Although every single misfortune appears as an exception, misfortune in general is the rule.[52] In this finite, ever-needy existence and in the constant state of unsatisfied striving, the will can never rest. Pain and sorrow are the necessary accompaniments of willing, and willing is our essence.

The secular objects of hope include not only the numerous wishes for the individual happiness of individuals, but values and norms of society or social groups. They too involve hope.

Marxist teachings emphasize the hope for revolution and liberation from bondage. Many movements and societies rely on values such as justice. Democracies, too, maintain their particular beliefs. Their fulfillment and continuity is connected with hope, which is also propagated among the people.

Already ancient Roman statesmen combined the values and institutions of their government with hope. They even had coins minted with their own portrait on the front and Spes, goddess of hope, engraved on the back. This was especially the hope for victories in military conflicts. Spes, the Roman equivalent of Elpis in Greek mythology, was portrayed as a tiptoeing girl, with a flower in her hand and often with a crow at her side, a symbol of permanence. The following coins show Commodus: as Caesar, 175-176 AD, with Spes on the back:

https://commons.wikimedia.org/wiki/File:
Commodus_Æ_As_175_732442.jpg[53]

Since the 5th century B.C., the personified hope was worshiped in Rome. The consul Gaius Horatius Pulvillus consecrated a temple on the Esquiline to Spes 477 B.C. after a victory over the Etruscans. In the middle of the 3rd century B.C. a temple on the Forum Holitorium (vegetable market) in Rome was consecrated to her by the consul Aulus Atilius Caiatinus. After the temple had been destroyed and rebuilt several times, the last inauguration took place in 17 B.C. by Germanicus.[54]

Remains of the temple of Spes,
Forum Holitorium in Rome[55]

In 2004, former Senator and later US President Barack Obama delivered a speech entitled "The Audacity of Hope" to the Democratic National Convention in Boston. He had taken the idea that hope was a venture from his former pastor Jeremiah Wright, who in turn, inspired by a lecture by Frederick G. Sampson in the late 1980s, had given a sermon on the painting "Hope" in 1990. Obama's core idea in his 2006 book *The Audacity Of Hope* is that all Americans are united by two basic values or beliefs, "freedom" and "community."

Interestingly enough, in the US, national self-understanding seems to include the belief that one lives in a free country, "land of the free, and home of the brave," as the American national anthem calls it. Nevertheless, freedom is presented here as the object of hope. The reason becomes clearer by an example that illustrates the personal freedom of employees in every day life. The big fish eat the little ones (Spinoza, *TTP*) and so freedom is reserved only for the strong, who are on the trigger and then even boldly demand that the weak should willingly let them eat them. We read in the employment contract of a contemporary American airline, "You agree to devote your full knowledge and entire working capacity to [the company]. Any side activities require the prior written consent of [the company]." This structure of imperialistic egoism demands the sacrifice of the renunciation of liberal self-realization. Forced one-dimensionality and / or imposed asceticism does not grant "exceptions" here, which are at least formally provided for in paragraph 73 of the

German Lower Saxon law for public servants of the state, the "Niedersächsisches Beamtengesetz." Otherwise, there is a similar restriction of side activities, and thus there is also a tendency to totally collect the serving individual.

3.2. Eternal Life

While secular thinking aims at personal contents of hope or social beliefs, and many ideologies even promise a paradise on earth, the transcendent hopes are for a heaven in the hereafter. The ethical individual is inclined to cherish hope for justice, if not in this life, then at least in an afterlife. For this purpose he must not only postulate a moral government of the world, but also hope for the immortality of the soul. Hell as described by Dante says, "Justice has brought me into being."

Twentieth century Christianity has further increased the positive evaluation of hope. Jürgen Moltmann defines hope as nothing but the expectation of those things which, according to faith, are truly promised by God.[56] The advice of Albert Camus, "to think clearly and no longer to hope," according to Moltmann". leads into the "utopia of the status quo." Albert Camus advocates reason, and prefers clear thought to mere hope; it is better to think more, and hope less. We should not waste our time on God as he is dead. Our fate is death, and hope is no comfort. But the experience of the absurd does not rule out any efforts to make sense. Camus says, "Where there is no hope, it is incumbent on us to invent it."[57]

But Moltmann also notes that those hoping for Christ begin to suffer from the given reality, for the sting of the promised future rages inexorably in the flesh of every unfulfilled present. However, transcendence should help to compensate for the shortage in this world, and so the Christian in his hope is freed from the need to secure his happiness here.[58] Ultimately, man hopes to know what he believes.[59]

In October 1994 the book of Pope John Paul II., *Crossing The Threshold of Hope*, appeared. There he emphasizes, God is the first source of joy and hope of man. The hope of victory over evil and death is reflected in the prayer for the suffering and the dead. It means that the church remains in the hope of eternal life.[60]

The transcendent variant of hope takes on a special position insofar as it can not really be disappointed because it is not falsifiable in life. However, faith can be disappointed if it is lost in conflict with knowledge.

Pascal (1623-1662) spoke of reasons of the heart (*raisons du coeur*) in religious context, and faith was seen in conflict with knowledge. But there were also attempts to reconcile belief and knowledge.

Kant (1724 - 1804) severed both sharply. He limited knowledge to gain a place for faith, but on the other hand he strove for a rational faith. Religious hopes of the beyond are rationalized by him, whereby his attempt at justification is based on the imperative of moral action, which should be more than mere matter of taste. In 1793, his work *Religion Within the Limits of Reason* appeared. On the one hand, he starts from the innate depravity of human nature, but on the other, he also relies on the ethical demand, which at the same time goes hand in hand with the possibility of the transformation of the heart into good.[61] Kant takes the view that man is completely denied self-knowledge in the sense of a clear insight into his own attitude.

Kant goes on to say that human natural innocence cannot be assumed, and that human reason always pleads against radical conversion and demanded self-perfection. Since, therefore, an incurable tendency to be immoral can be assumed, moral improvement can only be conceived as lying in an infinite approximation. What is required for this is a prior decision of the will, which becomes the steady, even immutable ground of all other decisions, the new heart. Kant denies man insight into the purity of his moral motivation, but along the way he must be able to hope to get there through his own exertion, because he should become a good person.[62] According to Kant, bliss would become exhausting because he thinks of it as an increase in rights and duties in the sense of self-optimization. And this would be a process ad infinitum without a foreseeable final goal or any point of rest or fulfillment. The one who is aware of going a long part of his life to the end of it, in the progress of improvement out of true moral motive, may have the consoling hope, if not certainty, that he, even in an existence continued beyond this life, will persevere in these principles and may look forward to a blissful future.[63]

In order for the ethical demand to act in such a way that one becomes worthy of being happy, does not remain meaningless and unfathomable, pure practical reason postulates God, freedom and the immortality of the soul.[64] These three metaphysical ideas of reason shall serve as guarantors that the moral hero is not a fool.[65] The corresponding religious hope does not found the action, but completes it.[66]

4. Intellectual Honesty

The one who strives for the truth must not subject this aspiration to the condition that the truth must also be useful, good or beautiful. But "what does the will to truth mean?" (Nietzsche) Wishful thinking sometimes has its justification. And not everyone wants to separate himself from his prejudices. Science and wisdom, truth and prudence are at times at war with each other. The true philosophy is not always the best. Philosophy not only destroys ideology, but also builds it. The greatest ideologues are philosophers.

But the truth makes you free. Man can liberate himself from errors made by wishes and hopes, by disciplining his judgment, by controlling his will to faith and keeping faith within the bounds of the understanding. Although a life lie may be useful and comforting, it is such only as long as it is believed to be true. An illusion is always exposed to possible discovery, and disappointed hope hurts. Hope is risky because it makes you vulnerable.

William James points out that both the rule of the cautious and the rule of the brave are tied to the passions. The skeptics are guided by the fear of error, the brave by the hope of winning. Therefore it is not the intellect that stands against the passions, but only one passion against another, namely fear against hope. Which is the better, is a decision that does not happen for logical reasons.[67] It is a matter of temperament.

Even our belief in the possibility of true knowledge and the pursuit of truth involves hope. Nietzsche (1844-1900) formulates this insight with regard to his "educator," "[...] our Schopenhauer: he had no hope, but he wanted the truth."[68]

Earlier, Spinoza had emphasized the influence of desire on the formation of judgment. Desire, whether conscious or unconscious, is grounded in the pursuit of self-preservation, which is inherent in every "thing."

In the *Tractatus Theologico-Politicus* and in *Ethics* he examines the prejudices. According to him, they are conditioned by the affects of joy and sadness, hope and fear, reassuring or suppressing, modifications of the survival instinct. Beliefs are for Spinoza. not a matter of free will as it was for his predecessor Descartes, but a matter of man's nature.

Nevertheless, he admits the possibility of adequate knowledge. We could look at things with the "eyes of God" and "from the point of view" of eternity, which means to comprehend the laws in nature. Our mind is designed to know the truth and can do so when its activity is pure.

4.1. Enlightenment

Concept and criticism of hope are the subject of any enlightenment. At the same time, the attempt to explain the compounds of hope and to show the scope and the limits of hope falls into the realm of criticism of ideology.

The so-called "enlightenment" was a rational project, while romanticism and pietism could be regarded as a countermovement. The enlightenment usually comprises certain thinkers and a program. In a narrow sense, it also denotes a historical epoch in the 18th century. In a broader sense of its intention, the enlightenment's beginnings can be seen within the natural sciences, linked to the name of Isaac Newton, in the humanities to John Locke, Condillac, Lessing, and in the social sciences to Turgot, Price und Rousseau. In general, reason should provide the foundation for an order of thinking and living, whereby mankind would progress in free necessity towards the true, the good, and happiness on earth. Faith in reason is combined with faith in a wise plan and government of the world, and purpose in history.

Kant defines the term "enlightenment" in an essay of 1784, as man's exit out of his immature intellectual dependency. We have been to blame for our laziness and lack of courage, and Kant tells us to take heart, and use our own brains.[69] Although Kant had rejected an optimism in the sense of Leibniz in the *Theodicy*, who asserted the prevalence of pleasure and believed in the bringing into being of the good through the bad, he nevertheless considered belief in a progression towards perfection as quite reasonable. He seeks to give hope a reasonable foundation. It is not only a consolation in life and counterbalance to its hardships, but results from the supposed certainty of our duty. So we may not only hope for God, freedom and immortality, but we would even have to rationally postulate these religious ideas for the sake of justice.

On an optimistic-religious ground, an explicit or implicit duty to happiness flourishes. Hope is not only the natural and original impulse of man, who has not been crushed by too many strokes of fate, but it is even religiously sanctioned and demanded. Therefore, every call to not give up hope is always willingly listened to, but it is usually only a mere echo of one's inner self. According to Schopenhauer, "it is natural for a man to have faith in what he wishes, and to have faith in it because he wishes it."[70]

With the exception of Kant, however, in the Age of Enlightenment a skeptical or negative attitude to hope prevails, as in Voltaire (1694-1778). In *Candide* he vehemently opposes the shallow optimism which has its basis in a lack of observation of the world and in Leibnizian *Theodicy*, i.e. the belief in this world as the best of all possible worlds. "What a life, one spends it hoping, only to end it with death, which in turn triggers more hope."

Similarly, Rousseau (1712-1778) emphasizes the personal disappointments, "I plant hope every day and see it wither every day."

Schopenhauer says:

> Life presents itself as a continual deception, in small matters as well as in great. If it has promised, it does not keep its word, unless to show how little desirable the desired object was; hence we are deluded now by hope.[71]

When hope not only expresses itself momentarily as an affect, but transforms itself into a constant attitude, a passion, then it manifests as optimism. Contemporary common sense defines an optimist as somebody who rather expects the good than the bad. It is somebody for whom a glass of water is half full instead of half empty as it appears to the pessimist.

The original meaning of optimism is different, though. The concept of optimism can be traced back to Leibniz who argues in his *Theodicy* that "this world is the best of all possible worlds" (*mundus optimus*). Optimism as a world view is derived from theology. For optimism the world – and God – is justified. In *Genesis* we read after each completed act of creation, "and God saw that it was good." If the Bible is considered as God's word and absolute truth beyond doubt, there is nothing bad about it, and it is blasphemy to point one's finger at it. Then man's task is to dance and be happy.

Schopenhauer sees misery as not only confined to mankind, but everywhere in nature. Every living being sustains its existence by devouring other life forms. Life is always destructive and necessarily at other beings' expense and agony.[72] And this is inevitable. While it is true that things like mountains and valleys, blooms and brooks etc. are pretty to *see*, it is a totally different story to *be* them. As a conclusion, Schopenhauer states the antithesis to Leibniz's thesis that this world is the best of all possible worlds, "This world is the *worst* of all possible worlds."[73] He stresses further that "*optimism*, where it is not merely the thoughtless talk of those who harbor nothing but words under their shallow foreheads, seems to me to be not merely an absurd, but also a really *wicked,* way of thinking, a bitter mockery of the unspeakable suffering of mankind."[74]

According to Schopenhauer, optimism is more typical and frequent in youth. Later in life modesty and worries dominate, caused by the many disappointments and bad experiences. During the first half of life we are longing for happiness, during the second half we are trying to avoid unhappiness.[75]

Not only do the different stages in life make a difference in susceptibility for optimism. Temper also is a factor. The realist is sober, while the optimist is enthusiastic. The melancholic, on the other hand, also has a selective perception like the optimist, but he picks the negative aspects instead of the positive ones from the spectrum. The optimist is carried away by hope, the melancholic by concern.[76] The optimist expects the best, the pessimist the worst. Whoever has no big expectations, rarely gets disappointed. Melancholy also involves a view distorted by encouragement. At a higher age and with more life experience, worldly wisdom usually increases and is characterized by more modest hopes.

4.2. Criticism of Ideology

Criticism of ideology, according to some contemporaries, is now superfluous, because there are no longer any ideologies in the sense of illusions. Ideologies are not cognitive errors, not "false consciousness" but, with reference to Louis Althusser", "lived relationships" and, in the same view of Terry Eagleton, they are not in the minds but in the institutions.[77]

The term "ideology" can be traced back to the French thinker Destutt de Tracy (1754-1836) who follows Locke and Condillac. It means the elucidation of the origins of ideas and structural foundations of state, society, church and other institutions. In this sense it is an investigation of ideas.

After Napoleon the term's meaning changes, and from that time until today denotes maladaptive rules, theories and programs which involve deceptive motives. To summarize, ideology is an interpretative scheme guided – often unconsciously - by interests. It may be introduced on purpose, to manipulate people in certain directions, and is likely to create "false consciousness" among its recipients. In this sense it can be regarded as a formation of an irrational belief system by means of apparently rational arguments, and deception of the mind. Man errs because he is satisfied by judgments without sufficient reason. If he fails to wake up from his "dogmatic slumber" (Kant) and thus remains intellectually immature, it is his own fault. But enlightenment is the way out. Critique of ideology aims to explain the fact of illusions, various handicaps of reasoning and flaws in thinking. It pertains not only to overt lies but also to the covert persuaders of human reason.[78]

Helvétius and Holbach are dedicated to unmasking prejudices. They see irrational repression in politics. Thomas Hobbes mentions the roles of hope and fear to manipulate people in this main work *Leviathan*.

Karl Marx (1818-1883) is regarded as the classical critic of ideology. He wants to turn Hegel upside down. He denies the primacy of reason. But Marx still had hope. He did not believe that man's consciousness determined his life, but on the contrary that his social environment determined his consciousness. In his opinion all that was needed was a change of the material situation to correct this false consciousness.

Schopenhauer disagrees with both Hegel and Marx. Each individual has to start at point zero. Everybody gets immersed in ideas produced by others before he can begin to use his own reason. Therefore enlightenment cannot only go on and on, but has to be starting anew all the time. And there must always be a distinction made between a critique of ideology, and an ideological critique. Namely, a critique is not immune to mystification either, and critical works have premises which have to be questioned, too. As diagnosed by Max Horkheimer and Theodor Adorno in the *Dialectic of Enlightenment* (1944), criticism has a tendency to turn into theory, and theory to turn into jargon. Some explanations which are satisfactory at a given time, may lose their explanatory and enlightening power over time because of changes in reality, and then they may become ideological theories themselves. If they are not questioned and put to the test, they prevent a fresh start to find a better explanation.

5. Intellectual Freedom

Immanuel Kant wrote three critiques as answers to basic human questions. These are fundamental questions of philosophy.[79] In 1781 the *Critique of Pure Reason* answers the question "what can I know?" *The Critique of Practical Reason* in 1788 treats the question "what should I do?" *The Critique of Judgment* in 1790 deals with the question of the beautiful and the sublime, and *Religion within the Boundaries of Mere Reason* in 1793 answers the question, "for what may I hope?"

Since the question is not what we *can* hope for, it can be assumed that the area of ability is greater than that of legitimacy. By legitimacy, Kant means the degree of rationality. Wishes and hopes can be the most improbable, but what may be hoped for reasonably good reason must meet certain rationality criteria and must not contradict reason. The meaning of "criticism" is to differentiate the more or less legitimate from the unjustified hopes.

How is intellectual freedom possible? Terry Eagleton says in *Hope without Optimism* that hope is a merit while optimism isn't. According to him, optimism is a mere natural trait, not any different from having red hair, for example. I disagree. If we have a choice at all, we can choose our emotions as much as we can choose our attitudes. Both are motivated by our experiences as well as our temper, though. So, optimism is encouraged by our successes in life, while failures will likely turn us towards pessimism.

Ideology criticism in the sense of recognition of interest refers both to self-knowledge and to knowledge of human nature. Man can be manipulated and remains a slave as long as he does not succeed in distinguishing the mirages from attainable goods. It is important to keep hope within the limits of reason. Kant points out, „One can remain safe from all error if one does not undertake to judge where one does not know what is required for a determinate judgment. Thus ignorance is in itself the cause for the limitations of our cognition, but not of the errors in it."[80]

The aim of Stoic ethics was a happy life. They had also learned from experience that "every wish soon dies and so can beget no more pain, if no hope nourishes it."[81] How do you live your life without being tormented by endless desire, fear and hope for things of little use?[82] Schopenhauer observes that while hopelessness is despair, "an unexpected misfortune is like a speedy death-stroke; while a hope that is always frustrated, and yet springs into life again, is like death by slow torture."[83]

Intellectual freedom means freedom from the blind effectiveness of the motives. Free is the one who is left unimpressed by all temptations. Above all, the "temptations of hope," which keep man in delusion and always seduce him to expect happiness in life, bind him the more firmly to suffering.[84]

The benefit of a critique of hope is to become as free as the sage can be. An inherent concept of salvation aims at satisfaction in life. A contribution to this is the attempt to limit hope by restricting desire to the conditions of reason. If you master this task, then philosophy may not yield you much benefit, but save you a lot of trouble.

Bibliography

Alighieri, Dante. *Die Göttliche Komödie.* München: DTV, [6]1992.

Aristoteles, *Die Nikomachische Ethik,* transl. And ed. Olof Gigon, München: DTV, [6]1986.

Aristoteles. *Hauptwerke.* Edited by W. Nestle. Stuttgart: Kröner, 1953.

Bahr, Ehrhard (Ed.) *Was ist Aufklärung?* Kant, Erhard, Hamann, Herder, Lessing, Mendelssohn, Riem, Schiller, Wieland. Stuttgart: Reclam, 1981.

Barth, Hans. „Schopenhauers ‚Eigentliche Kritik der Vernunft'. In: *Schopenhauer.* Edited by Jörg Salaquarda. Darmstadt: Wissenschaftliche Buchgesellschaft, 1985, 60-72. (Wege der Forschung; 602).

Bloch, Ernst. *Das Prinzip Hoffnung.* Werkausgabe Band 5. Frankfurt/M.: Suhrkamp, 1959.

Brügger, Peter. „Die radikale Unvernunft der menschlichen ‚Vernunft' – Schopenhauers Beitrag zur Ideologiekritik." *Schopenhauer-Jahrbuch* 66 (1985), 53-257.

Dahl, Edgar (Ed.). *Die Lehre des Unheils: Fundamentalkritik am Christentum.* Hamburg: Carlsen, 1993.

Descartes, René. *Die Prinzipien der Philosophie.* Translated and annotated by Artur Buchenau. - Hamburg: Meiner, [7]1965. (Philosophische Bibliothek; 28).

Descartes, René. *Die Leidenschaften der Seele.* Hamburg: Meiner, 1984. (Philosophische Bibliothek; 345.)

Descartes, René. *Meditationen über die Erste Philosphie.* Translated and annotated by Gerhart Schmidt. Stuttgart: Reclam, 1983.

Eagleton, Terry. *Hope without Optimism.* University of Virginia Press, 2015.

Eagleton, Terry. *Ideology: An Introduction.* London/ New York: Verso, 1991.

Eisler, Rudolf (Ed.). *Wörterbuch der philosophischen Begriffe.* Berlin: Mittler u. Sohn, [4]1927. („Hoffnung" p. 637.)

Fahrenbach, H. *Wesen und Sinn der Hoffnung.* Diss. Heidelberg 1956.

Haffmans, Gerd (Ed.). *Das Schopenhauer Nachschlag-Werk: Ein*

Abc für die Jetztzeit, nebst einem Anhang, der die Kritik der korrupten Vernunft enthält. Zürich: Haffmans, 1989.

Horkheimer, Max. „Die Aktualität Schopenhauers." (1961). In: *Zur Kritik der instrumentellen Vernunft.* Edited by Alfred Schmidt. Frankfurt: Fischer TB, 1985, 248-268.

Hübscher, Arthur. *Denker gegen den Strom. Schopenhauer: gestern – heute – morgen.* Bonn: Bouvier, 1973.

Hume, David: *A Treatise of Human Nature: Being an Attempt to Introduce the Experimental Method of Reasoning into Moral Subjects*, London 1739/40, Reprint Oxford 1968.

James, William. „The Will to Believe", in: *The Will to Believe and other essays in popular philosophy. Human Immortality,* both books bound as one, New York: Dover Publ., 1956.

Kant, Immanuel. *Critique of Pure Reason.* Translated, edited and with an Introduction by Marcus Weigelt. Penguin Classics, 2007.

Kant, Immanuel. *Critique of Practical Reason.* Translated and edited by Mary Gregor. Cambridge University Press, 2015.

Kant, Immanuel. *Critique of Judgement.* Translated by James Creed Meredith. New York: Oxford University Press, 2007.

Kant, Immanuel. *Religion within the Boundaries of Mere Reason and other Writings.* Translated and edited by Allen Wood and George di Giovanni. Cambridge University Press, [17]2016.

Kant, Immanuel. *Kritik der praktischen Vernunft.* Edited by Joachim Kopper. Stuttgart: Reclam, 1992.

Kant, Immanuel. *Kritik der reinen Vernunft.* Edited by Ingeborg Heidemann. Stuttgart: Reclam, 1966. Repr. 1982.

Kant, Immanuel. *Kritik der Urteilskraft.* Edited by Gerhard Lehmann. Stuttgart: Reclam, 1963. Repr. 1981.

Kant, Immanuel. *Die Religion innerhalb der Grenzen der bloßen Vernunft.* Edited by Rudolf Malter. Stuttgart: Reclam, 1981.

Kerstiens, Ferdinand. *Die Hoffnungs-struktur des Glaubens*. Mainz: Matthias-Grünewald-Verlag, 1969.

Klencke, Hermann. *Pessimismus und Schopenhauer mit Bezug auf Spinoza als Heilmittel des Pessimismus*. Leipzig: 1882.

Kliemt, Hartmut. „Der Glaube als Feind der Aufklärung". In: *Die Lehre des Unheils: Fundamentalkritik am Christentum*. Edited by Edgar Dahl. Hamburg: Carlsen, 1993.

Krings, Hermann et al. (Ed.). *Handbuch philosophischer Grundbegriffe*. Bd. II. München: Kösel-Verlag, 1973. („Hoffnung" pp. 692-700.)

Lehmann, Rudolf. *Schopenhauer: Ein Beitrag zur Psychologie der Metaphysik*. Berlin: Weidemann, 1894.

Malter, Rudolf: 'Eine wahrhaft ruchlose Denkungsart': Schopenhauers Kritik der Leibnizschen Theodizee. In: *Studia Leibnitiana* XVIII/2 (1986), 152-182.

Marcel, Gabriel. *Homo viator. Philosophie der Hoffnung*. Düsseldorf: Bastion, 1949.

Marcuse, Ludwig. *Philosophie des Glücks: Von Hiob bis Freud.* Zürich: Diogenes, 1972.

Marcuse, Ludwig. *Unverlorene Illusionen. Pessimismus – ein Stadium der Reife.* München: Szczesny, [2]1966.

Middendorf, Heinrich. *Phänomenologie der Hoffnung.* Amsterdam: Rodopi, Würzburg: K&N, 1985. (Elementa: ; 40).

Moltmann, Jürgen. *Theologie der Hoffnung: Untersuchungen zur Begründung und zu den Konsequenzen einer christlichen Eschatologie.* München: Kaiser, 1968. (Beiträge zur evangelischen Theologie, Theologische Abhandlungen; 38).

Nietzsche, Friedrich. *Kritische Gesamt-Ausgabe.* Edited by Giorgio Colli und Mazzino Montinari, Berlin/New York 1967 ff.

Nietzsche, Friedrich. Zur Genealogie der Moral. *Werke* III. Edited by Karl Schlechta. Repr. [6]1969. Frankfurt: Ullstein, 1979.

Nietzsche, Friedrich. Das Verhältnis der schopenhauerschen Philosophie zu einer deutschen Kultur. In: *Werke* Bd. III. Edited by Karl

Schlechta. Frankfurt am Main 1979, 995-998.

Nietzsche, Friedrich. *Jenseits von Gut und Böse: Vorspiel einer Philosophie der Zukunft*. München: Goldmann, (Goldmann Klassiker ; 7530).

Obama, Barack. *The Audacity of Hope. Thoughts on Reclaiming the American Dream*. New York: Crown/Three Rivers Press 2006.

Pope Johannes Paul II. *Die Schwelle der Hoffnung überschreiten*. Edited by Vittorio Messori. Translated by Irene Esters. Hamburg: Hoffmann und Campe, [2]1994.

Pisa, Karl. *Schopenhauer: Kronzeuge einer unheilen Welt*. Wien/ Berlin: Neff, 1977.

Ritter, Joachim (Ed.). *Historisches Wörterbuch der Philosophie*. („Hoffnung" pp. 1157-1166.)

Rorty, Richard. *Philosophy and Social Hope*. Penguin, 1999.

Schmidt, Alfred. *Die Wahrheit im Gewande der Lüge: Schopenhauers Religionsphilosophie.* München: Piper, 1986.

Schopenhauer, Arthur. "Aphorisms on the Wisdom of Life", chap. 5, "Counsels and Maxims", in: *Parerga and Paralipomena,* Vol. 1; Oxford, England: Oxford University Press, first published 1974; reissued 2000, p. 408. Translated by E.F.J. Payne.

Schopenhauer, Arthur. *On the Sufferings of the World.* Transl. by T. Bailey Saunders, http://www. - readbookonline. net/readOnLine/- 22579/.

Schopenhauer, Arthur. "Psychological Observations" by Arthur Schopenhauer, transl. R. Dircks, http:// ebooks. adelaide. edu.au/s/scho- penhauer/arthur/essays/chapter9. html.

Schopenhauer, Arthur. *Sämtliche Werke.* Ed. Wolfgang Frh. von Löhneysen. 5 Bände. - Darmstadt: Wissenschaftliche Buchgesellschaft, repr. ²1989.

Schopenhauer, Arthur. *The World as Will and Representation.* Vol. I. Translated from the German by E.F.J. Payne. New York: Dover Publications, 1969.

Schopenhauer, Arthur. *The World as Will and Representation.* Vol. II. Translated from the German by E.F.J. Payne. New York: Dover Publications, 1958.

Schopenhauer, Arthur. *Werke in zehn Bänden*. Zürcher Ausgabe. Zürich: Diogenes, 1977.

Schottlaender, Rudolf. „Die Freiheit des Wesens. Spinozas Umdeutung von Glaube, Hoffnung und Liebe." *Frankfurter Allgemeine Zeitung* 24.11.1982.

Schulz, Ortrun. *Schopenhauer's Critique of Hope*. Norderstedt: BoD, 2014.

Schulz, Ortrun. „Die Kritik der Hoffnung bei Spinoza und Schopenhauer." *Schopenhauer-Jahrbuch* 80 (1999), 125-145.

Spinoza, Baruch de. *Abhandlung über die Verbesserung des Verstandes. Abhandlung vom Staate*. Hamburg: Meiner, [5]1977 (Philosophische Bibliothek; 95.)

Spinoza, Baruch de. *Die Ethik; Schriften und Briefe*. Edited by Friedrich Bülow. – Repr. [7]1976. Stuttgart: Kröner, 1982. (Kröners Taschenausgabe; 24).

Spinoza, Baruch de. *Descartes' Prinzipien der Philosophie auf geometrische Weise begründet*. Mit dem „Anhang, enthaltend metaphysische Gedanken."

Translated by Artur Buchenau. Hamburg: Meiner, 1987. (Philosophische Bibliothek; 94).

Spinoza, Baruch de. *Kurze Abhandlung von Gott, dem Menschen und seinem Glück*. Edited by Carl Gebhardt. Hamburg: Meiner, repr. 1965.

Windelband, Wilhelm. *Die Geschichte der neueren Philosophie*, Bd. II. Leipzig 1880.

Wren, T.E. "Is Hope a necessary Evil? Some Misgivings about Spinoza's metaphysical Psychology." *Journal of Thought* 7 (1972), pp. 67-76.

Index

Notes

[1] Quoted by Arthur Schopenhauer, *The World as Will and Representation* I, First Book, §16, translated by E.F.J. Payne, New York: Dover 1969, p. 90.

[2] Page URL: https:// commons.wikimedia.org/wiki/File%3AAssistants_and_George_Frederic_Watts_-_Hope_-_Google_Art_Project.jpg, File URL: https:// upload.wikimedia.org/wikipedia/commons/e/eb/Assistants_and_George_Frederic_Watts_-_Hope_-_Google_Art_Project.jpg.

[3] George Frederic Watts [Public domain], via Wikimedia Commons.

[4] Schopenhauer, *Parerga und Paralipomena* II, Einige mythologische Betrachtungen, § 200, Löhneysen Werke V, pp. 486-7.

[5] *Historisches Wörterbuch der Philosophie*, Band 3, edited by Joachim Ritter, Darmstadt: Wissenschaftliche Buchgesellschaft, 1974, pp. 1157ff.

[6] *Historisches* Wörterbuch *der Philosophie*, Band 3, edited by Joachim Ritter, Darmstadt: Wissenschaftliche Buchgesellschaft, 1974, pp. 1157-1166.

[7] Aristoteles, *Rhetorik* II, 5, 1382a 21; II, 12, 1389a 20ff.

[8] https://de.wikipedia.org/wiki/Drei_heilige_Frauen.

9 https://commons. wikimedia.org/wiki/-File: Sophia_mit_ihren_3_Kindern.JPG. By Altera levatur (Own work) [CC BY-SA 4.0 (https://creativecommons.org/licenses/by -sa/4.0)], via Wikimedia Commons.

10 *Handbuch philosophischer Grundbegriffe*, edited by H. Krings et al., München: Kösel, 1973, p. 692.

11 *Handbuch philosophischer Grundbegriffe*, p. 694.

12 René Descartes, *Die Leidenschaften der Seele*, Hamburg: Meiner, 1984, (Philosophische Bibliothek ; 345.), 2. Teil, Artikel 58, p. 99.

13 Spinoza, Baruch de. *Die Ethik; Schriften und Briefe*, edited by Friedrich Bülow. – Repr. 71976. Stuttgart: Kröner, 1982, p. 126, E3Prop12. Also E3Prop25.

14 Spinoza, E3, Kröner, p. 132. Cf. the definitions of affects, p. 177.

15 Spinoza, E4Prop47, Kröner, p. 236.

16 Spinoza, E4Prop47Schol, Kröner, p. 237.

17 Spinoza, E3Prop50, Kröner, p. 159.

18 Spinoza, Baruch de. *Abhandlung über die Verbesserung des Verstandes. Abhandlung vom Staate*. Hamburg: Meiner, 51977 (Philosophische Bibliothek; 95.) Abhandlung vom Staate (Tractatus politicus) 2/10, Meiner p. 64.

19 Wren, T.E. "Is Hope a necessary Evil? Some Misgivings about Spinoza's

metaphysical Psychology." *Journal of Thought* 7 (1972), p. 70.

[20] Ernst Bloch, *Das Prinzip Hoffnung*. Werkausgabe Band 5. Frankfurt/M.: Suhrkamp, 1959, p. 74.

[21] Schopenhauer, *Parerga und Paralipomena* II, Psychologische Bemerkungen, § 324a, Löhneysen Werke V, p. 693.

[22] Schopenhauer, *Parerga und Paralipomena* II, Psychologische Bemerkungen, § 348, Löhneysen Werke V, p. 709.

[23] Schopenhauer, *Parerga und Paralipomena* II, Zur Lehre vom Leiden der Welt, Löhneysen Werke V, p. 349.

[24] Schopenhauer, *Parerga und Paralipomena* II, Zur Lehre vom Leiden der Welt, Löhneysen Werke V, p. 349.

[25] Schopenhauer, *The World as Will and Representation* II, Chap. XIX, On the Primacy of the Will in Self-Consciousness, Dover, p. 216.

[26] Schopenhauer, *Die Welt als Wille und Vorstellung* II, 2. Buch, Kap. 19, Vom Primat des Willens im Selbstbewußtsein, Löhneysen Werke II, p. 282.

[27] Schopenhauer, *The World as Will and Representation* II, Chap. XIX, On the Primacy of the Will in Self-Consciousness, Dover, p. 217-8.

28 Schopenhauer, *The World as Will and Representation* II, Chap. XIX, Dover, p. 218.

29 Schopenhauer, *Parerga und Paralipomena* II, Den Intellekt betreffende Gedanken, Löhneysen Werke V, p. 81.

30 http://ebooks.adelaide.edu.au/s/schopenhauer/arthur/essays/chapter9. html, "Psychological Observations" by Arthur Schopenhauer, translated by Mrs. R. Dircks. Cf. Schopenhauer, *Parerga und Paralipomena* II, Psychologische Bemerkungen, § 313, Löhneysen Werke V, p. 688.

31 Schopenhauer, *The World as Will and Representation* II, Chap. XIX, On the Primacy of the Will in Self-Consciousness, Dover, p. 217-8.

32 Gabriel Marcel, *Homo viator. Philosophie der Hoffnung.* Düsseldorf: Bastion, 1949, p. 63.

33 Schopenhauer, *Parerga und Paralipomena* II, Psychologische Bemerkungen, § 314, Löhneysen Werke V, p. 688. Cf. also Schopenhauer, *The World as Will and Representation* II, Chap. XIX, On the Primacy of the Will in Self-Consciousness, Dover, pp. 220f.

34 Schopenhauer, *The World as Will and Representation* II, Chap. XXII, Objective View of the Intellect, Dover, p. 280.

35 Ernst Bloch, *Das Prinzip Hoffnung.* Werkausgabe Band 5. Frankfurt/M.: Suhrkamp, 1959, pp. 1-3.

36 Dante Alighieri, *Die Göttliche Komödie*, München: DTV, 61992. Hölle, III. Gesang, p. 16.

37 Dante Alighieri, *Die Göttliche Komödie*, Hölle, V. Gesang, p. 26.

38 By Wikinaut (Own work) [CC BY-SA 3.0 (https://creativecommons.org/licenses/by-sa/3.0) or GFDL (http://www.gnu.org/-copyleft/fdl.html)], via Wikimedia Commons.

39 *Handbuch philosophischer Grundbegriffe*, edited by Hermann Krings et al., München: Kösel, 1973, p. 693.

40 Heinrich Middendorf, *Phänomenologie der Hoffnung*, Amsterdam: Rodopi, Würzburg: K&N, 1985, (Elementa ; 40), p. 6, 13.

41 Spinoza, *E*3P9S.

42 Ludwig Marcuse, *Philosophie des Glücks*, 1972, p. 167.

43 Spinoza, *E*5P15.

44 Friedrich Nietzsche, *Jenseits von Gut und Böse: Vorspiel einer Philosophie der Zukunft*, 7. Hauptstück: „Unsere Tugenden", 217, München: Goldmann, (Goldmann Klassiker ; 7530), p. 109.

45 Spinoza, *E*5P18S.

[46] Ludwig Marcuse, *Unverlorene Illusionen. Pessimismus - ein Stadium der Reife*, München: Szczesny, 1966, p. 157.

[47] Ludwig Marcuse, *Unverlorene Illusionen. Pessimismus - ein Stadium der Reife*, München: Szczesny, 1966, p. 157.

[48] Rudolf Malter, „'Eine wahrhaft ruchlose Denkungsart': Schopenhauers Kritik der Leibnizschen Theodizee", *Studia Leibnitiana* XVIII/2 (1986), p. 180.

[49] Arthur Schopenhauer, "Aphorisms on the Wisdom of Life", chap. 5, "Counsels and Maxims", *Parerga and Paralipomena*, Vol. 1; Oxford, England: Oxford University Press, first published 1974; reissued 2000, p. 408. Translated by E.F.J. Payne.

[50] Arthur Schopenhauer, Kap. 12, „Nachträge zur Lehre vom Leiden der Welt", P II, Löhneysen Werke V, p. 348; 349; 351.

[51] Ibid., p. 344.

[52] Ibid., p. 343.

[53] By Classical Numismatic Group, Inc. http://www.cngcoins.com, CC BY-SA 2.5, https://commons.wikimedia.org/w/index.php?curid=10602939.

[54] https://de.wikipedia.org/wiki/Spes.

[55] https://de.wikipedia.org/wiki/Spes#/-media/File: Rom_BW_1.JPG, https:// de. - wikipedia.org/wiki/Spes.

[56] Jürgen Moltmann, *Theologie der Hoffnung: Untersuchungen zur Begründung*

und zu den Konsequenzen einer christlichen Eschatologie, München: Kaiser, 1968, p. 16. (Beiträge zur evangelischen Theologie, Theologische Abhandlungen; 38).

[57] Cf. Albert Camus, *Der Mensch in der Revolte*. Essays, Hamburg: Rowohlt, 1953, pp. 28f.

[58] Ferdinand Kerstiens, *Die Hoffnungs-struktur des Glaubens*, Mainz: Grünewald, 1969, p. 208.

[59] Moltmann, p. 28.

[60] Johannes Paul II, *Die Schwelle der Hoffnung überschreiten*, p. 53.

[61] Immanuel Kant, *Die Religion innerhalb der Grenzen der bloßen Vernunft*, edited by Rudolf Malter, Erstes Stück, Allgemeine Anmerkung, Stuttgart: Reclam, 1981, p. 64.

[62] Immanuel Kant, *Die Religion innerhalb der Grenzen der bloßen Vernunft*, p. 65.

[63] Immanuel Kant, *Kritik der praktischen Vernunft*, edited by Joachim Kopper, Stuttgart: Reclam, 1992, p. 196-7 footnote.

[64] Immanuel Kant, *Kritik der praktischen Vernunft*, p. 210.

[65] Immanuel Kant, *Kritik der praktischen Vernunft*, p. 206.

[66] Immanuel Kant, *Kritik der praktischen Vernunft*, p. 196.

[67] William James, „The Will to Believe", in: *The Will to Believe and other essays in*

popular philosophy. Human Immortality, both books bound as one, New York: Dover Publ., 1956, p. 27.

68 Friedrich Nietzsche, *Kritische Gesamt-Ausgabe,* edited by Giorgio Colli and Mazzino Montinari, Berlin/New York 1967 ff., 3,1, Aph. 20, p. 127.

69 *Was ist Aufklärung?* Edited by Ehrhard Bahr, Stuttgart: Reclam, 1981, pp. 8-9.

70. http://ebooks.adelaide.edu.au/s/schopenhauer/arthur/essays/chapter9.html, "Psychological Observations" by Arthur Schopenhauer, transl. Mrs. Rudolf Dircks. Cf. Schopenhauer, *Parerga und Paralipomena* II, Psychologische Bemerkungen, § 313, Löhneysen *Werke* V, p. 688.

71 Schopenhauer, *The World as Will and Representation* II, Chap. XLI, On the Vanity and Suffering of Life, Dover, p. 573.

72 Schopenhauer, *The World as Will and Representation* I, §58, The Assertion and Denial of the Will to Live, Dover, p. 325.

73 Schopenhauer, *The World as Will and Representation* II, Chap. XLVI, On the Vanity and Suffering of Life, Dover, p. 583.

74 Schopenhauer, *The World as Will and Representation* I, §59, p. 326.

75 Schopenhauer, *Der handschriftliche Nachlaß,* Bd. 3: Berliner Manuskripte (1818-1830), edited by Arthur Hübscher,

München: DTV, 1985, Reisebuch (1822?), Nr. 142, p. 58.

[76] Schopenhauer, *The World as Will and Representation* II, Chap. XIX, On the Primacy of the Will in Self-Consciousness, Dover, p. 280.

[77] Terry Eagleton, *Ideology: An Introduction*, London/ New York: Verso, 1991, pp. 38; 40.

[78] Cf. Peter Brügger, „Die radikale Unvernunft der menschlichen ‚Vernunft' – Schopenhauers Beitrag zur Ideologiekritik", in: 66. *Schopenhauer-Jahrbuch* (1985), p. 254.

[79] Immanuel Kant, *Critique of Pure Reason*, A805/B833.

[80] Immanuel Kant, *Reason within the Boundaries of Mere Reason*, translated and edited by Allen Wood and George di Giovanni, Cambridge University Press, [17]2016, p.6.

[81] Schopenhauer, *The World as Will and Representation* I, Book I, §16, Dover, p. 87.

[82] Schopenhauer, *The World as Will and Representation* I, Book I, §16, Dover, p. 90.

[83] http://ebooks.adelaide.edu.au/s/schopenhauer/arthur/essays/chapter9.html, "Psychological Observations" by Arthur Schopenhauer, translated by Mrs. Rudolf Dircks. Cf. Schopenhauer, *Parerga und Paralipomena* II, Psychologische Bemer-

kungen, § 313, Löhneysen Werke V, p. 688.

84 Schopenhauer, *W* I(2), Diogenes p. 485.